asha

A Child of the Himalayas

By Céline Castelain and
Aurélien Liutkus

BLACKBIRCH PRESS

An imprint of Thomson Gale, a part of The Thomson Corporation

THOMSON
GALE

Detroit • New York • San Francisco • San Diego • New Haven, Conn. • Waterville, Maine • London • Munich

© Éditions PEMF, 2001

First published by PEMF in France as *Asha, enfant d'Himalaya*.

First published in North America in 2005 by Thomson Gale.

For more information, contact
Blackbirch Press
27500 Drake Rd.
Farmington Hills, MI 48331-3535
Or you can visit our Internet site at http://www.gale.com

Photo Credits: All photos © Céline Castelain and Aurélien Liutkus except pages 6, 9 Corel Corporation; Table of Contents collage: EXPLORER/Boutin (upper left); François Goalec (upper middle and right); Muriel Nicolotti (bottom left); CIRIC/Michel Gauvry (bottom middle); CIRIC/Pascal Deloche (bottom right)

LIBRARY OF CONGRESS CATALOGING-IN-PUBLICATION DATA

Castelain, Céline.
  Asha : a child of the Himalayas / by Céline Castelain and Aurélien Liutkus.
    p. cm. — (Children of the world)
  ISBN 1-4103-0286-5 (hardcover : alk. paper)
  1. Himachal Pradesh (India)—Juvenile literature. 2. Children—India—Himachal Pradesh—Juvenile literature. I. Castelain, Céline II. Liutkus, Aurélien. II. Title. III. Series: Children of the world (Blackbirch Press)

  DS485.H5C38 2005
  954'.52035—dc22
                             2005000695

Printed in the United States of America
10 9 8 7 6 5 4 3 2 1

Contents

Facts About Himachal Pradesh, India

Himachal Pradesh is part of India. India is an immense country about five times the size of Texas. Himachel Pradesh became an official state of India in 1971.

Agriculture:	rice and various fruits
Capital:	Simla
Government:	democracy
Land Area:	21,496 square miles (55,673 square kilometers)
Languages:	Hindi, English, and Pahari
Population:	5,600,000
Religions:	Hinduism and Buddhism

The Land of Eternally Snowy Peaks

The Himalayan Mountains remain covered in snow throughout the year.

Himachal Pradesh is one of the highest regions of the world. Called the "Land of Eternally Snowy Peaks," the region includes the mountains of the Himalayan chain, between Pakistan and Tibet.

Himachal Pradesh means "State of the Mountains." In this region, the mountains are often as high as 16,400 feet (5,000 meters).

Above: Peppers dry in the sun.

7

The Village of Naggar

Naggar is the former capital of the Himalayas, or the Valley of the Gods. Today it is a charming little village perched on a hill.

The lower part of the village is made up of streams, orchards, and farmland.

Wildlife lives in the surrounding forests of Naggar. Brown bears, monkeys, and jackals live side by side with many kinds of snakes, including the frightening python. The Naggar people respect all wildlife.

Bottom Right: The Himalayan Tahr

Below: A Rhesus monkey

Asha and Her Family

Asha is a seven-year-old girl from the mountains. She was born in Naggar. She lives with her mother, Mena, and two sisters, Pudja and Oucha.

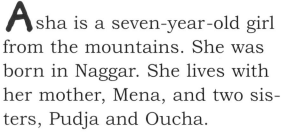

Asha stands between her two sisters. Pudja, fourteen, wears the blue uniform reserved for older girls. Oucha is eight years old. Their mother, Mena, takes care of her three daughters.

Above: Asha's uncle stands on the balcony of their house.

Below: Asha's house has only one room. Asha and her mother share the same bed. Pudja and Oucha sleep on a mat on the floor.

Asha's house is made of wood and stone. At the moment, the roof is in bad shape. The family does not have enough money to replace it.

Asha, her sisters, and her mother share the same room that also serves as their living room and dining room.

Asha's Daily Life

Asha and her sisters love to play in the forest. They gather flowers and drink the icy cold water of the mountain streams.

After school, they must help their mother prepare the meal and bring the water.

Above: Asha and Oucha make garlands of flowers. They will offer them to gods in the temple.

Right: There is no running water in the house. Asha's family must bring it from the river.

The family must prepare dinner before nightfall because there is no electricity in the house.

In India, most children know how to cook by the age of ten. Evenings are spent around the fire, where the parents tell stories of marvelous legends.

Below: In the kitchen, Mena prepares dal, a traditional Indian meal made of lentils and dried beans cooked into a sauce. She also makes pancakes called chapati. And don't forget the chai, tea with milk and spices.

Above: The family garden produces some impressive vegetables.

13

On the Way to School

Not all children in India are able to go to school. Asha, Pudja, and Oucha know this and would not be late for anything in the world.

To get to school, the three sisters take a spectacular path that winds through the middle of the forest. Sometimes they come across a few cows. These animals are sacred in India.

Below: "Who will take care of India and Himachal Pradesh?"

"We will take care of them," the students respond together.

Above: Every morning the students line up and sing in the courtyard of their school. School begins at ten o'clock.

Before entering the classroom, the students have an exercise period. Then they salute their nation and promise to take care of their parents when they are old.

15

At School

At ten o'clock in the morning, the students begin their day. They study subjects such as Hindi, mathematics, and English. There are about 50 students in a class.

Above: Asha and her friends.

Right: Two teachers sit with a few of their students.

Asha and her classmates will not have desks until they are in the eleventh grade, at the age of fifteen.

Right: Boys and girls are in the same class.

भारतीय स्वतंत्रता संग्राम का इतिहास भाग-5

0506

हिमाचल प्रदेश स्कूल शिक्षा बोर्ड, धर्मशाला

A history book written in Hindi.

Businesses and Small Trades

The stonecutter.

Small market stalls are set up throughout Naggar. There are no big stores. Life is organized around the weaver, the stonecutter, and the baker.

The market of Naggar. Vessels are sold for carrying water to the homes.

Above: The weaver.

Below: A rickshaw waits for passengers.

Above: A woman carries cut grass in a basket on her back.

To get around in the village and even farther, people sometimes hire a rickshaw. They are not very big, but Indians try to stuff in four, five, or sometimes even more passengers!

19

Religion

Naggar is a village where tradition plays a big role in daily life.

The villagers gather regularly around the temple where a god resides.

The village's Hindu temple is in front of the school.

Everything is sacred in India, and the gods are respected.

Behind the wooden doors is the statue of a god. During religious festivals, it is lifted on a stretcher, decorated with colored cloths, and carried throughout the village.

Religious Festivals

Even the days of the week are under the gods' influence. On Tuesday, the day of the monkey-god Hanuman, it is better not to cut one's hair or beard.

The men of the village wear the topi, or the traditional hat, as they parade through the streets of the village during a festival.

22

Wednesday, the day of the elephant-god Ganesh, is a lucky day. Saturday is a day to be on one's guard.

During religious festivals, the streets of the village are adorned with garlands and streamers.

Other Books in the Series

Arafat: A Child of Tunisia

Avinesh: A Child of the Ganges

Ballel: A Child of Senegal

Basha: A Hmong Child

Frederico: A Child of Brazil

Ituko: An Inuit Child

Kradji: A Child of Cambodia

Kuntai: A Masai Child

Leila: A Tuareg Child

Madhi: A Child of Egypt

Thanassis: A Child of Greece

Tomasino: A Child of Peru